BOSTON COMMON PRESS
Brookline, Massachusetts

1999

Boston Common Press
17 Station Street
Brookline, Massachusetts 02445

ISBN 0-936184-30-2
Library of Congress Cataloging-in-Publication Data
The Editors of *Cook's Illustrated*

How to cook shrimp and other shellfish: An illustrated step-by-step guide to preparing shrimp, scallops, clams, mussels, oysters, lobster, and crabs./The Editors of *Cook's Illustrated*
1st ed.

Includes 43 recipes and 30 illustrations
ISBN 0-936184-30-2 (hardback): $14.95
I. Cooking. I. Title
1999

Manufactured in the United States of America

Distributed by Boston Common Press, 17 Station Street, Brookline, MA 02445.

Cover and text design: Amy Klee
Recipe development: Dawn Yanagihara
Series editor: Jack Bishop

HOW TO COOK SHRIMP & OTHER SHELLFISH

An illustrated step-by-step guide to
preparing shrimp, scallops, clams, mussels,
oysters, lobster, and crabs.

THE COOK'S ILLUSTRATED LIBRARY

Illustrations by John Burgoyne

CONTENTS

introduction

L IKE MANY HOME COOKS, I OFTEN ORDER FISH when I go out to eat since I find that restaurants are more apt to procure really fresh specimens than I am. Good meat is both easier to come by and also more forgiving if it is not perfectly fresh. Nonetheless, shrimp and shellfish such as clams, oysters, mussels, scallops, lobster, and even crab are widely available, and most are still alive when sold. Although this does not guarantee freshness, it does substantially increase the odds in your favor. The problem is, how do you cook them?

Having performed hundreds of hours of tests in our kitchen, we present in these pages those cooking methods which work best. Although one can broil, grill, or even oven-roast scallops with some success, our testing revealed that pan-searing and deep-frying deliver the best results. Therefore, we have restricted our coverage to those cooking methods. We have tried just about every method imaginable to guarantee tender lobster meat, including preparing them in every season of the year; we have taste-tested every major variety of oyster to help you choose the ones you will like best; and, for shrimp, we have tested when to shell them before cooking and whether deveining is necessary. And we found a big difference between hard- and soft-shell clams. The soft-shells are gritty and very hard to clean, so it pays to purchase the hard-shell variety.

Our hope is that our discoveries will take a bit of the mystery out of preparing shrimp and shellfish and put some of the fun back in.

We have also published *How to Make a Pie, How to Make an American Layer Cake, How to Stir-Fry, How to Make Ice Cream, How to Make Pizza, How to Make Holiday Desserts, How to Make Pasta Sauces, How to Make Salad, How to Grill, How to Make Simple Fruit Desserts, How to Make Cookie Jar Favorites, How to Cook Holiday Roasts and Birds,* and *How to Make Stew.* Many other titles in this series will soon be available. To order other books, call us at (800) 611-0759. We are also the editors and publishers of *Cook's Illustrated,* a bimonthly publication about American home cooking. For a free trial copy of Cook's, call (800) 526-8442.

Christopher P. Kimball
Publisher and Editor
Cook's Illustrated

chapter one

❧

SHRIMP

COOKING SHRIMP IS A RELATIVELY STRAIGHT-forward process. As soon as the meat turns pink (which can happen in just two or three minutes over intense heat), the shrimp are done. How the shrimp are handled before cooking actually generates more confusion. Should they be peeled? Should the vein that runs down the back of each shrimp be removed?

There are two basic ways of cooking shrimp, either with dry heat (for example, grilling or pan-searing) or moist heat (for example, poaching or steaming). After some initial tests, we concluded that shrimp must be prepared differently when cooked by dry and moist heat. We found that when shrimp are grilled or pan-seared, the shell shields the meat from the intense heat and helps to keep the shrimp moist and tender. Try as we might, we found it impossible to grill or pan-sear peeled shrimp without overcooking them and making the meat dry and tough, especially the exterior layers. The only method that worked was to intentionally undercook the shrimp; but that left the inside a little gooey, something that almost no one enjoyed.

When shrimp are cooked in liquid the tables turn, and it is best to peel them first. The exterior of shrimp cooked in liquid are not as prone to drying out, and the shells can be simmered in the liquid to increase its flavor. Also, it is nearly impossible to peel shrimp cooked in hot liquid. While the peel separates easily from grilled or pan-seared shrimp, the shells become firmly attached to the meat when the shrimp are cooked in liquid.

In addition to peeling, the issue of deveining generates much controversy among experts. Although some people won't eat shrimp that has not been deveined, others believe that the "vein"—actually the animal's intestinal tract—contributes flavor and insist on leaving it in. In our tests, we could not detect an effect (either positive or negative) on flavor when we left the vein in. The vein is generally so tiny in most medium-sized shrimp that it virtually disappears after cooking. Out of laziness, we leave it alone. In larger shrimp, the vein is usually larger as well. Very large veins can detract from the overall texture of the shrimp and are best removed before cooking.

One more step worth taking when preparing shrimp for dry cooking is to brine them in a salt solution. Brining causes shrimp to become especially plump (they may gain as much 10 percent in water weight) and firm. The science is fairly simple. Salt causes protein strands in the shrimp to unwind, allowing them to trap and hold onto more moisture when cooked. At its most successful, brining turns mushy shrimp into shrimp with the chewy texture of a lobster tail. Even top-quality shrimp are improved by this process. We tested various concentrations of salt and brining times, and in the end settled on soaking shrimp in a strong salt solution (three cups kosher salt dissolved in five and one-half cups water) for 20 to 25 minutes.

Once the shrimp has been brined, it can be dumped into a hot skillet or threaded onto skewers and grilled. Unpeeled shrimp is easy to cook either way. As soon as the meat turns pink, the shrimp are done. We found that shrimp should be cooked quickly to prevent them from toughening. This means using a very hot skillet or a hot grill fire.

When pan-searing, it's easy enough to make a quick pan sauce once the shrimp have been cooked and transferred to a bowl. Just add some oil and seasonings (garlic, shallots, lemon juice, herbs, spices) to the empty pan and cook briefly. The sauce can then be tossed with the shrimp in the shell to coat them. When grilling, we like to coat the shrimp with a paste or marinade before cooking. With both pan-searing and grilling, the flavorings adhere to the shell beautifully. When you peel the shrimp at the table, the seasonings stick to your fingers and they are in turn transferred directly to the meat as you eat it. Licking your fingers also helps.

When poaching shrimp for cocktail or salad, brining is not necessary—the shrimp remain nice and plump when cooked in liquid. The issue here is how to flavor the shrimp as it cooks. If you start with good shrimp and simmer them in salted water until pink, the shrimp will have a decent but rarely intense flavor. Cooking them in their shells (which actually contain a lot of the "briny" flavor we associate with good seafood) helps improve the flavor of the shrimp, but the cooked shrimp are very hard to peel. When steamed, the shells attach to the meat, and it becomes hard to remove them without tearing the meat below. In addition, we found that it takes a good 20 minutes for the shells to give up their flavor. Clearly, the shrimp meat will be long overcooked by this time.

Our solution is to peel the shrimp and simmer the shells alone with the salted water to make a quick stock. To give the stock even more flavor, we tried adding other ingredients to the strained stock. After trying a dozen different combinations, involving wine, vinegar, lemon juice, and various herbs and spices, we found that a mixture of three parts quick shrimp stock to one part white wine, with a dash of lemon juice and some traditional herbs (bay leaf, parsley, and tarragon) does the best job of flavoring the shrimp as it cooks. At higher concentrations, the wine and lemon juice are too overpowering.

At this point in our testing, we liked the flavor of our poached shrimp but wondered if prolonging the cooking time (and hence the time the shrimp was in contact with the flavorful broth) would improve its flavor. We tried lowering the heat but found that it was too easy to overcook the shrimp and make it tough. What worked best was to bring the broth to a boil, turn off the heat, add the shrimp, and cover the pot. The shrimp can stay in the liquid for 10 minutes or so (as opposed to just 2 or 3 minutes if the liquid is boiling), enough time to really pick up the flavor of the liquid.

In addition to dry-heat cooking or poaching, there are two other cooking methods for shrimp worth considering. True shrimp scampi contains peeled pink shrimp floating in plenty of garlicky sauce that can be used to moisten bread or rice. The challenge is cooking the shrimp in a skillet in such a way that will produce these wonderful juices.

We added every liquid we could think of—white wine,

lemon juice, fish and chicken stock, even water—but were disappointed. Olive oil didn't work either. The wine and lemon juice added too much acidity, extra oil made the dish greasy, and the stocks and water diluted the flavor of the shrimp. During these tests, we also noticed that an overly high heat makes the garlic too brown and also toughens the shrimp.

When we lowered the heat the liquid given up by the shrimp lingered in the pan. We set out to cook the shrimp more slowly, in effect braising it in olive oil and its own natural juices. Because our goal was to preserve the liquid and tenderness of the shrimp rather than create crispness, the technique is closer to braising than sautéing.

Once we started to move in this direction, everything fell into place. With lower heat, the garlic becomes tender and mellow, the olive oil retains its freshness, and the shrimp remains moist and tender.

Our last experiments involved deep-frying shrimp. We tested a variety of coatings and preferred a simple one made with bread crumbs. It was crisp and crunchy (we found that a crunchy coating offers a nice contrast with tender shrimp and other shellfish), and it browns nicely. When we tried dredging the shrimp in flour then dipping it in egg and rolling it in bread crumbs, the coating separated from the shrimp. We preferred just egg and then bread crumbs since the coating rests right on the shrimp and offers the best contrast in textures. Cornmeal lacked the same crunch and color. A beer batter was too puffy and light, and the beer flavor detracted from the seafood flavor. Also, the beer batter is not at all crunchy but soft. A mixture of flour and milk made a pasty coating with no crunch, and adding some egg to the batter didn't do much to improve it.

As for the frying medium, we found that peanut and corn oil were the most flavorful. Canola and vegetable oil were fine, if less flavorful.

A final note about buying shrimp. There are more than 300 species of shrimp grown around the world. (There is such a thing as "wild" shrimp, but most shrimp is farm-raised.) Black tiger shrimp from Asia is the most common variety sold in U.S. markets. It can be firm and tasty, but the quality is inconsistent. In our taste tests, we preferred Mexican whites from the Pacific Coast and Gulf whites. They were the firmest and had the strongest fresh-from-the-sea flavor. However, we didn't like all the white shrimp we tasted. Chinese white shrimp were decidedly inferior to both the Mexican and Gulf white shrimp and to most of the tiger shrimp.

In general, the flavor and texture differences in various species are most noticeable when shrimp is poached and used in shrimp cocktail. Our advice is simple: If you have a choice, look for white shrimp from Mexico or the Gulf, especially when making shrimp cocktail.

Master Recipe

Brined Shrimp

➤ **NOTE:** *When pan-searing or grilling, we recommend that you brine the shrimp first to make them especially plump and juicy.*

    3   **cups kosher salt or 2 cups table salt**
    2   **pounds large shrimp (21 to 25 count**
        per pound)

INSTRUCTIONS:

Pour 2 cups boiling water into large bowl. Add salt, stirring to dissolve, and cool to room temperature. Add 3½ cups ice water and shrimp and let stand 20 to 25 minutes. Drain and rinse thoroughly under cold running water. Open shells with manicure scissors (*see* figure 1, page 17) and devein if desired (*see* figure 2, page 17).

▪▪ VARIATION:

Brined Frozen Shrimp

In many ways, uncooked frozen shrimp offer consumers the best quality since the shrimp are frozen at sea and then thawed at home, not at the market, as is the case with almost all the "fresh" shrimp sold at the retail level. However, because frozen shrimp are generally sold in five-pound blocks, these shrimp can be difficult to handle. Rather than trying to saw through a block of ice, we recommend putting the frozen block of shrimp under cold running water and pulling off individual shrimp as they become free. When you have the desired amount of shrimp (in this recipe, two pounds), place the remaining portion of the block back in the freezer and proceed with brining the partially thawed shrimp.

Follow Master Recipe, using 3½ cups cold (not ice) water since the shrimp themselves are still partially frozen. Proceed as directed with brining.

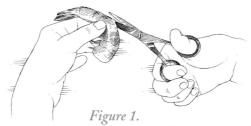

Figure 1.

When cooked with dry heat (pan-searing or grilling), shrimp are best cooked in their shells. The shells hold in moisture and also flavor the shrimp as they cook. However, eating shrimp cooked in its shell can be a challenge. As a compromise, we found it helpful to slit the back of the shell with a manicure or other small scissors with a fine point. After cooking, each person can quickly and easily peel away the shell.

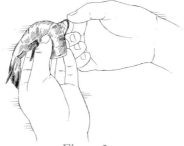

Figure 2.

Slitting the back of the shell makes it easy to devein the shrimp as well. Except when the vein is especially dark and thick, we found no benefit to deveining in our testing. If you choose to devein shrimp, slit open the back of the shell (figure 1). Invariably you will cut a little into the meat and expose the vein as you do this. Use the tip of the scissors to lift up the vein, and then grab it with your fingers and discard.

Master Recipe

Pan-Seared Shrimp

➤ **NOTE:** *This recipe delivers shrimp in its simplest and purest form. The variations add some other flavors but are also remarkably simple. To keep burnt bits from ending up in the sauce, rinse and wipe clean the pan after the shrimp has been cooked. Serves four to six.*

1   recipe Brined Shrimp (page 15)
½   lemon

■ INSTRUCTIONS:

1. Heat large nonstick or cast-iron skillet over high heat until very hot. Place single layer of shrimp in pan. Cook until shrimp shells turn spotty brown, 1 to 2 minutes. Turn shrimp as they brown; cook until remaining side turns spotty brown, 1 to 2 minutes longer. As shrimp are done, transfer them to medium bowl. Repeat process with remaining shrimp.

2. Squeeze lemon juice over shrimp and serve warm or at room temperature.

⠿ VARIATIONS:

Pan-Seared Shrimp with Shallots and Tarragon

Follow Master Recipe through step 1. Omit lemon. Rinse and wipe out pan with paper towel. Heat 1 tablespoon olive oil in skillet over medium heat. Add 1 large minced shallot and sauté until softened and just beginning to brown, 1 to 1½ minutes; add to bowl with shrimp. Add 1½ tablespoons sherry vinegar, 1½ tablespoons minced fresh tarragon leaves, and salt and ground black pepper to taste to bowl. Toss to combine.

Pan-Seared Shrimp with Southwestern Flavors

Follow Master Recipe through step 1. Omit lemon. Rinse and wipe out pan with paper towel. Heat 1 tablespoon olive oil in skillet over medium heat. Add 1 large minced garlic clove, 2 teaspoons chili powder, and ¾ teaspoon ground cumin and sauté until garlic is fragrant and lightens in color, 30 to 45 seconds; add to bowl with shrimp. Add 2½ table-spoons lime juice, 2 tablespoons minced fresh cilantro leaves, and salt and ground black pepper to taste to bowl. Toss to combine.

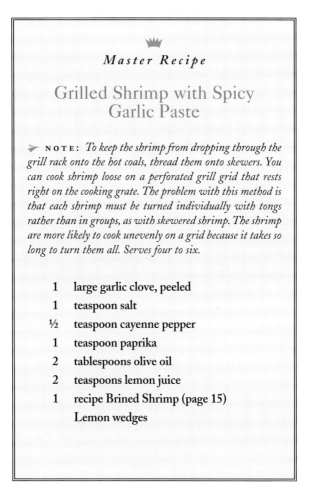

♛

Master Recipe

Grilled Shrimp with Spicy Garlic Paste

➤ **NOTE:** *To keep the shrimp from dropping through the grill rack onto the hot coals, thread them onto skewers. You can cook shrimp loose on a perforated grill grid that rests right on the cooking grate. The problem with this method is that each shrimp must be turned individually with tongs rather than in groups, as with skewered shrimp. The shrimp are more likely to cook unevenly on a grid because it takes so long to turn them all. Serves four to six.*

1	large garlic clove, peeled
1	teaspoon salt
½	teaspoon cayenne pepper
1	teaspoon paprika
2	tablespoons olive oil
2	teaspoons lemon juice
1	recipe Brined Shrimp (page 15)
	Lemon wedges

♔
Master Instructions

1. Light grill. Mince garlic with salt into smooth paste. Mix garlic and salt with cayenne and paprika in small bowl. Add oil and lemon juice to form thin paste. Toss shrimp with paste until evenly coated. (Can be covered and refrigerated for up to 1 hour). Thread shrimp onto skewers (*see* figure 3, page 23).

2. Grill shrimp over medium-hot fire, turning once (*see* figure 4, page 23), until shells are bright pink, 2 to 3 minutes per side. Serve hot or at room temperature with lemon wedges.

⠿ VARIATIONS:

Broiled Shrimp

Follow Master Recipe, adjusting oven rack to top position. Place skewered shrimp in jelly roll or other shallow pan and broil, turning once, until shells are bright pink, 2 to 3 minutes per side.

Grilled or Broiled Shrimp with Asian Flavors

Unlike the garlic paste (which adheres beautifully to the shrimp as they cook), this seasoning mixture is fairly liquid and falls off. We found that letting the shrimp sit in this mixture for at least half an hour (but no more than an hour) flavors them nicely.

Follow Master Recipe, omitting all ingredients except brined shrimp. Combine 1½ tablespoons soy sauce, 2 teaspoons rice wine vinegar, ¾ teaspoon Asian sesame oil, 1½ teaspoons sugar, ½ teaspoon grated fresh gingerroot, 1 large minced garlic clove, and 2 minced scallions in medium bowl. Toss shrimp with mixture and let marinate 30 to 60 minutes. Skewer and grill, or broil as directed.

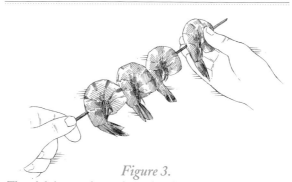

Figure 3.

Thread shrimp on skewers by passing the skewer through the body near the tail, folding the shrimp over, and passing the skewer through the shrimp again near the head. Threading each shrimp twice keeps it in place (it won't spin around) and makes it easy to cook the shrimp on both sides by turning the skewer just once.

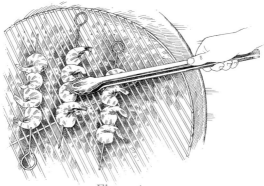

Figure 4.

Long-handled tongs make it easy to turn hot skewers on the grill. Lightly grab onto a single shrimp to turn the entire skewer.

✦

Master Recipe

Herb-Poached Shrimp

➤ **NOTE**: *If using larger or smaller shrimp, increase or decrease cooking times for shrimp by a minute or two. There is no need to use manicure scissors to open the shells since they should be completely removed before cooking in liquid. Simply open the shells with your fingers under running water and slip them off the meat. If you want to remove the vein, slit the back of each shrimp with a paring knife and rinse under cold water to wash away the vein. If possible, use Mexican or Gulf white shrimp in this recipe.*

1	pound large shrimp (21 to 25 count per pound), peeled, deveined if desired, and rinsed, shells reserved
1	teaspoon salt
1	cup dry white wine
4	peppercorns
5	coriander seeds
½	bay leaf
5	sprigs fresh parsley
1	sprig fresh tarragon
1	teaspoon lemon juice

♔
Master Instructions

1. Bring reserved shells, 3 cups water, and salt to boil in medium saucepan over medium-high heat. Reduce heat to low, cover, and simmer until fragrant, about 20 minutes. Strain stock through sieve, pressing on shells to extract all liquid.

2. Bring stock and remaining ingredients except shrimp to boil in 3- to 4-quart saucepan over high heat. Boil for 2 minutes. Turn off heat and stir in shrimp. Cover and let stand until firm and pink, 8 to 10 minutes. Drain shrimp, reserving stock for another use, such as in pasta sauce or fish stew or soup. Plunge shrimp into ice water to stop cooking, then drain again. Refrigerate shrimp and proceed with cocktail or salad recipe.

Shrimp Cocktail

➤ **NOTE:** *We prefer cocktail sauce that starts with ketchup rather than bottled chili sauce, which is generally too vinegary. The cocktail sauce benefits from a variety of heat sources, none of which overpowers the others. For best flavor, use horseradish from a fresh bottle and mild chili powder. Serves four as an appetizer.*

1	cup ketchup
2½	teaspoons prepared horseradish
¼	teaspoon salt
¼	teaspoon ground black pepper
1	teaspoon ancho or other mild chili powder
	Pinch cayenne
1	tablespoon lemon juice
	Crushed ice
1	recipe Herb-Poached Shrimp (page 24), chilled

INSTRUCTIONS:

1. Stir all ingredients except ice and shrimp together in small bowl. Adjust seasonings.

2. Fill four goblets with crushed ice. Arrange shrimp over ice, with tails hanging over sides of goblets. Serve immediately with cocktail sauce.

♛

Master Recipe

Shrimp Salad

➤ NOTE: *This salad makes an excellent filling for soft rolls. If serving this salad over greens, slice the shrimp in half lengthwise rather than chopping them coarse. Serves four.*

1   recipe Herb-Poached Shrimp (page 24), chopped very coarse
1   medium celery rib, cut into small dice
1   medium scallion, white and green parts, minced
⅓   cup mayonnaise
1   tablespoon lemon juice
1   tablespoon minced fresh parsley leaves
    Salt and ground black pepper

⦂ INSTRUCTIONS:

Mix all ingredients together in medium bowl, including salt and pepper to taste. Serve. (Can be covered and refrigerated overnight.)

■■ VARIATIONS:

Shrimp Salad with Chipotle Chile

Follow Master Recipe, adding 1 small chipotle chile in adobo, minced, with all ingredients, and substituting lime juice for lemon and fresh minced cilantro leaves for parsley.

Curried Shrimp Salad

Follow Master Recipe, adding 1 teaspoon curry powder with all ingredients.

♛

Master Recipe

Shrimp Scampi

➤ **NOTE:** *Use the cayenne pepper sparingly to give the faintest hint of spiciness. Serves four.*

- ¼   cup extra-virgin olive oil
- 4   medium garlic cloves, minced
- 2   pounds large shrimp (21 to 25 count per pound), peeled, deveined if desired, and rinsed
- ¼   cup minced fresh parsley leaves
- 2   tablespoons lemon juice
     Salt
     Cayenne pepper to taste

INSTRUCTIONS:

Heat oil and garlic in 10-inch skillet over medium heat until garlic begins to sizzle. Reduce heat to medium-low and cook until fragrant and pale gold, about 2 minutes. Add shrimp, increase heat to medium, and cook, stirring occasionally, until shrimp
(Continued on next page)

♛

Master Instructions

(Continued from previous page)

turn pink, about 7 minutes. Be careful not to overcook shrimp or they will become tough. Off heat, stir in parsley, lemon juice, and salt and cayenne pepper to taste. Serve immediately.

▪ VARIATIONS:

Shrimp Scampi with Cumin, Paprika, and Sherry Vinegar

Follow Master Recipe, sautéing 1 teaspoon ground cumin and 2 teaspoons paprika with garlic, substituting an equal amount of sherry vinegar for lemon juice, and omitting cayenne.

Shrimp Scampi with Orange Zest and Cilantro

Follow Master Recipe, sautéing 1 teaspoon finely grated orange zest and ¼ teaspoon hot red pepper flakes with garlic, substituting 2 tablespoons minced fresh cilantro leaves for parsley, and omitting cayenne.

Fried Shrimp

➤ **NOTE:** *We hate to waste oil when frying. For that reason, we like to fry shrimp and other shellfish in batches in a four-quart saucepan filled with just 5 cups of oil. Serves four as an appetizer, two as a main course.*

1	large egg
½	teaspoon salt
	Ground black pepper
¾	cup plain dry bread crumbs
1	pound shrimp, peeled, deveined if desired, and rinsed
	About 5 cups peanut or corn oil for frying
	Lemon wedges or Tartar Sauce (page 92)

INSTRUCTIONS:

1. Beat egg with salt and pepper to taste in small bowl. Place bread crumbs in wide, shallow dish. Working several at a time, dip shrimp in egg mixture, shake off excess, then coat with bread crumbs, pressing to make crumbs adhere. Set shrimp on cookie sheet; repeat with remaining shrimp.

2. Heat 1½ inches of oil in heavy 4-quart saucepan to 360 degrees. Add half of shrimp and fry until deep golden brown, about 60 seconds. Remove with slotted spoon and drain on double layer of paper towels on cooling rack. Repeat with remaining shrimp, letting oil come back up to temperature if necessary. Serve with lemon wedges or tartar sauce.

chapter two

SCALLOPS

S CALLOPS OFFER SEVERAL POSSIBLE CHOICES FOR the cook, both when shopping and cooking. There are three main varieties of scallops—sea, bay, and calico. Sea scallops are available year-round throughout the country and are the best choice in most instances. Like all scallops, the product sold at the market is the dense, disk-shaped muscle that propels the live scallop in its shell through the water. The guts and roe are usually jettisoned at sea because they are so perishable. Ivory-colored sea scallops are usually at least an inch in diameter (and often much bigger) and look like squat marshmallows. Sometimes they are sold cut-up, but we found that they can lose moisture when handled this way and are best purchased whole.

Small, cork-shaped bay scallops (about half an inch in diameter) are harvested in a small area from Cape Cod to Long Island. Bay scallops are seasonal—available from late fall through midwinter—and are very expensive, up to $20 a pound. They are delicious but nearly impossible to find outside of top restaurants.

Calico scallops are a small species (less than half an inch across and taller than they are wide) harvested in the southern United States and around the world. They are inexpensive (often priced at just a few dollars a pound) but generally not terribly good. Unlike sea and bay scallops, which are harvested by hand, calicos are shucked by machine steaming. This steaming partially cooks them and give them an opaque look. Calicos are often sold as "bays," but they are not the same thing. In our kitchen test, we found that calicos are easy to overcook and often end up with a rubbery, eraser-like texture. Our recommendation is to stick with sea scallops, unless you have access to real bay scallops.

In addition to choosing the right species, you should inquire about processing when purchasing scallops. Most scallops (by some estimates up to 90 percent of the retail supply) are dipped in a phosphate-and-water mixture that may also contain citric and sorbic acids. Processing extends shelf life but harms the flavor and texture of the scallop. Its naturally delicate, sweet flavor can be masked by the bitter-tasting chemicals. Even worse, scallops absorb water during processing, which is thrown off when they are cooked. You can't brown processed scallops in a skillet—they shed so much liquid that they steam.

By law, processed scallops must be identified at the wholesale level, so ask your fishmonger. Also, look at the scallops. Scallops are naturally ivory or pinkish tan; process-ing turns them bright white. Processed scallops are slippery and swollen and usually sitting in milky white liquid at the store. Unprocessed scallops (also called dry scallops) are sticky and flabby. If they are surrounded by any liquid (and often they are not), the juices are clear, not white.

Besides the obvious objections (why pay for water weight or processing that detracts from their natural fla-vor?), processed scallops are more difficult to cook. We found that sautéing to carmelize the exterior to a concen-trated, nutty flavored, brown and tan crust is the best way to cook scallops. The caramelized exterior greatly enhances the natural sweetness of the scallop and provides a nice crisp contrast with the tender interior.

The most common problem a cook runs into with scal-lops is getting a nice crust before the scallop overcooks and toughens. We started our tests by focusing on the fat in the pan. Since scallops cook quickly, we knew it would be important to choose a fat that browns efficiently. We tried butter, olive oil, canola oil, a combination of butter and oil, plus cooking in oil with a finish of butter at the end for flavor.

To preserve the creamy texture of the flesh, we cooked the scallops to medium-rare, which means the scallop is hot all the way through but the center still retains some translucence. As a scallop cooks, the soft flesh firms and you can see an opaqueness that starts at the bottom of the scallop, where it sits in the pan, and slowly creeps up toward the center. The scallop is medium-rare when the sides have firmed up and all but about the middle third of the scallop has turned opaque.

The scallops browned well in all the fats we tested, but butter produced the thickest crust and best flavor. The nutty taste of butter complements the sweetness of the scallop without compromising its delicate flavor. We tested various pans, and while the technique worked in both nonstick and regular skillets, we recommend a light-colored regular skillet so you can judge how quickly the butter is browning and regulate the heat if necessary.

Despite the origin of the word *sauté,* which means "to jump" in French, it's critical for the formation of a good crust to leave the scallop alone once it hits the pan. We found the best method for cooking was to place the scallops carefully in the pan one at a time, with one flat side down for maximum contact with the hot pan. We turned the scallops once and browned the second flat side. The best tool for turning scallops is a pair of tongs, although a spatula can be used in a pinch.

We recommend pan-searing in butter as the best all-purpose method for cooking scallops. Like shrimp, scallops can also be breaded and deep-fried. While the preparation is simple (just remove the small muscle on each side of the scallop), frying the scallops presented more of a problem than we thought they would in our testing.

We tried simply breading and frying sea scallops, but differing sizes caused trouble. The big ones didn't cook through before they became too dark. We tried using calicos instead. They were a pain to dredge because they are so small, and they became tough when cooked. We went back to frying sea scallops, slicing them in half at the equator, and although this improved their cooking, they lost some appeal as flat discs. So we opted to leave the small ones (about 1 inch in diameter and ¾ inch high) whole. If you can only buy larger scallops, cut them in half vertically, or in quarters if the scallops are really quite large (more than 1½ inches in diameter).

⬤ Master Recipe

Pan-Seared Scallops

➤ NOTE: *This recipe was developed for standard sea scallops, about the size of a short, squat marshmallow. If using smaller scallops, turn off the heat as soon as you turn them; they will finish cooking from the residual heat, 15 to 30 seconds longer. For very large scallops, turn the heat to low once they have browned and continue cooking for 1 minute. Then turn the scallops, raise the heat to medium, and cook them at least 2 minutes on the second side. Serves four.*

1½   pounds sea scallops (about 30 to a pound),
      small muscles removed (*see* figure 5,
      page 40)
      Salt and ground black pepper
1½   tablespoons unsalted butter

▦ INSTRUCTIONS:

1. Sprinkle scallops on both sides with salt and pepper to taste. Heat an 11-inch sauté pan over medium-high heat until hot, about 1 minute. Add half the

(*Continued on next page*)

♛

Master Instructions

(Continued from previous page)

butter; swirl to coat pan bottom. Continue to heat pan until butter begins to turn golden brown.

2. Add half the scallops, one at a time, flat side down. Cook, adjusting heat as necessary to prevent fat from burning, until scallops are well browned, 1½ to 2 minutes. Using tongs (*see* figure 6, page 40), turn scallops, one at a time. Cook until medium-rare (sides have firmed up and all but middle third of scallop is opaque), 30 to 90 seconds longer, depending on size. Transfer scallops to warm platter; cover with foil. Repeat cooking process using remaining butter and scallops. Serve immediately.

VARIATIONS:

Pan-Seared Scallops with Lemon, Shallots, and Capers

Follow Master Recipe. After searing scallops and transferring to platter, pour off all but 1 tablespoon butter and sauté 1 medium minced shallot in fat until softened, 1 to 2 minutes. Add 1 cup dry white wine and 1 teaspoon grated lemon zest, and simmer until reduced to about ⅓ cup, 6 to 7 minutes. Off heat, stir in 2 tablespoons unsalted butter, 2 tablespoons minced fresh parsley leaves, 1 tablespoon lemon juice, 1 tablespoon minced capers, and salt and pepper to taste. Spoon sauce over scallops and serve.

Pan-Seared Scallops with Sherry, Red Onion, Orange, and Thyme

Follow Master Recipe. After searing scallops, and transferring to warm platter, pour off all but 1 tablespoon butter and sauté ⅓ cup minced red onion in fat until softened, 1 to 2 minutes. Add ¾ cup dry sherry, ¼ cup orange juice, 1 teaspoon grated orange zest, and 1 teaspoon minced fresh thyme, and simmer until reduced to about ⅓ cup, 6 to 7 minutes. Off heat, stir in 2 tablespoons unsalted butter, 1 tablespoon lemon juice, and salt and pepper to taste. Spoon sauce over scallops and serve.

Figure 5.
The small, rough-textured, crescent-shaped muscle that attaches
the scallop to the shell is often not removed during processing. You
can readily remove any muscles that are still attached. If you
don't, they will toughen slightly during cooking.

Figure 6.
When sautéing scallops, make sure not to overcrowd the skillet or they
will not brown properly. Use tongs to turn the scallops in the pan.

40

Fried Scallops

➤ **NOTE**: *Small sea scallops are best because they will cook through before the coating burns. If scallops are larger than 1 inch in diameter and ¾ inch high, they should be cut vertically in half before breading. Jumbo scallops (more than 1½ inches in diameter) should be quartered vertically. Serves four as an appetizer, two as a main course.*

    1   large egg
         Salt and ground black pepper
    ½   cup plain dry bread crumbs
    1   pound sea scallops, halved or quartered if
         necessary (*see* note)
         About 5 cups peanut or corn oil for frying
         Lemon wedges or Tartar Sauce (page 92)

▪▪ **INSTRUCTIONS:**

1. Beat egg with salt and pepper to taste in small bowl. Place bread crumbs in wide, shallow dish. Working several at a time, dip scallops in egg mixture, shake off excess, then coat with bread crumbs, pressing to make crumbs adhere. Set scallops on cookie sheet; repeat with remaining scallops.

2. Heat 1½ inches of oil in heavy 4-quart saucepan to 360 degrees. Add half of scallops and fry until deep golden brown, about 60 seconds. Remove with slotted spoon and drain on double layer of paper towels on cooling rack. Repeat with remaining scallops, letting oil come back up to temperature if necessary. Serve with lemon wedges or tartar sauce.

chapter three

3

CLAMS AND MUSSELS

THE REAL CHALLENGE WHEN PREPARING clams and mussels is getting rid of the grit. These two-shelled creatures are easy to cook: When they open, they are done. However, perfectly cooked clams and mussels can be made inedible by lingering sand. Straining their juices through cheesecloth after cooking will remove the grit, but it's a pain. Besides being messy, solids such as shallots and garlic are removed. Worse still, careful straining may not remove every trace of grit, especially bits that are still clinging to the clam or mussel meat.

After much trial and error in the test kitchen, we concluded that it is also impossible to remove all the sand from dirty clams or mussels before cooking. We tried various soaking regimens—such as soaking in cold water for two hours, soaking in water with flour, soaking in water with cornmeal, and scrubbing and rinsing in five changes of water. None of these techniques worked. Dirty clams and mussels must be rinsed and scrubbed before cooking, and any cooking liquid must be strained after cooking. Rinsing the cooked clams and mussels is a final guarantee that the grit will be removed, but flavor is washed away as well.

During the course of this testing, we noticed that some varieties of clams and mussels were extremely clean and free of grit. A quick scrub of the shell exterior and these bivalves were ready for the pot. Best of all, the cooking liquid could be served without straining. After talking to seafood experts around the country we came to this conclusion: If you want to minimize your kitchen work and ensure that your clams and mussels are free of grit, you must shop carefully.

Clams can be divided into two categories—hard-shell varieties (such as littlenecks and cherrystones) and soft-shell varieties (such as steamers and razor clams). Hard-shells grow along sandy beaches and bays; soft-shells in muddy tidal flats. A modest shift in location makes all the difference in the kitchen.

When harvested, hard-shells remain tightly closed. In our tests, we found the meat inside to be sand-free. The exterior should be scrubbed under cold running water to remove any caked-on mud, but otherwise these clams can be cooked without further worry about gritty broths.

Soft-shell clams gape when they are alive. We found that they almost always contain a lot of sand. While it's worthwhile to soak them in several batches of cold water to remove some of the sand, you can never get rid of it all. In the end, you must strain the cooking liquid. People often rinse clams once more at the table in individual bowls of broth.

We ultimately concluded that hard-shell clams (that is, littlenecks or cherrystones) are worth the extra money at the market. Gritty clams, no matter how cheap, are inedible. Buying either littlenecks or cherrystones ensures that the clams will be clean.

A similar distinction can be made with mussels based on how and where they are grown. Most mussels are now farmed either on ropes or along seabeds. (You may also see "wild" mussels at the market. These mussels are harvested the old-fashioned way—by dredging along the sea floor. In our tests, we found them to be extremely muddy and basically inedible.) Rope-cultured mussels can cost twice as much as wild or bottom-cultured mussels, but we found them to be free of grit in our testing. Since mussels are generally inexpensive (no more than a few dollars a pound), we think clean mussels are worth the extra money. Look for tags, usually attached to bags of mussels, that indicate how and where the mussels have been grown.

When shopping, look for tightly closed clams and mussels (avoid any that are gaping; these may be dying or dead). Clams need only be scrubbed. Mussels may need scrubbing as well as debearding. Simply grab onto the weedy protrusion and pull it out from between the shells and discard. Don't debeard mussels until you are ready to cook them, as debearding can cause the mussel to die. Mussels or clams kept in sealed plastic bags or under water will also die. Keep them in a bowl in the refrigerator and use them within a day or two for best results.

We tested the four most common cooking methods for clams and mussels: steaming in an aromatic broth (usually with some wine in it), steaming in a basket set over an aromatic broth, roasting in the oven, and sautéing in some oil on the stove. In our tests, we found that clams or mussels that were sautéed, roasted, or steamed over a broth tasted of pure shellfish, but they also tasted flat and one-dimensional. They cooked in their juices. In contrast, clams and mussels that were steamed in a flavorful broth picked up flavors from the liquid. They became more complex tasting and, in our opinion, better.

45

With steaming in broth as our preferred all-purpose cooking method, we started to test various amounts and types of liquids, including fish stock, water, wine, and beer. We found white wine to be the best choice, although beer worked nicely with the mussels and is given as an option on page 51. The bright acidity of white wine balances the briny flavor of clams and mussels. Fish stock and water (even when seasoned with garlic, herbs, and spices) were dull by comparison. While it is possible to steam four pounds of bivalves in just half a cup of liquid (naturally, the pot must be tightly sealed), we like to have extra broth for soaking into bread or rice. We settled on using two cups of white wine to cook four pounds of clams or mussels.

We also made some refinements to the cooking broth. Garlic, shallots, and a bay leaf enrich the flavor of the shellfish. Simmering the broth for three minutes before adding the shellfish is sufficient time for these seasonings to flavor the wine broth. The all-purpose broth can be flavored in numerous ways, as the recipe variations in this chapter demonstrate.

As an aside, we also tested grilling clams and mussels, a method that has become popular in recent years. We also tested frying clams. Neither method can be considered all-purpose, but each has its advantages. Although delicious, fried clams are too much work for the average home cook.

Using preshucked clams delivers mediocre results, and shucking clams yourself is an arduous task. Leave fried clams to restaurants.

Grilling is an interesting idea, especially for summer entertaining. Steaming is clearly the easiest and best way to cook clams and mussels, but because grilling is such a novelty and the results can be quite good, we decided to include a recipe in this chapter. If you are cooking outside and want to throw a few clams or mussels over the coals to serve as an appetizer, we think you will be pleased with the results. We found it is important not to move the shellfish around on the grill and to handle them carefully once they open. You want to preserve as much of the natural juice as possible, so when the clams or mussels open, transfer them with tongs to a platter, holding them steady so as not to tip out any of the liquid.

♛

Master Recipe

Steamed Clams or Mussels

➤ **NOTE:** *The basic flavorings in this recipe work with all kinds of mussels and with either littlenecks or cherry-stone clams. (Really large cherrystones may require 9 or 10 minutes of steaming to open.) Variations below may be better suited to the particular flavor of mussels or clams as indicated. Serves four as a main course with woarm bread or rice, eight as an appetizer.*

- **2** cups white wine
- **2** large shallots (½ cup minced)
- **4** medium garlic cloves, minced
- **1** bay leaf
- **4** pounds clams or mussels, scrubbed and debearded if cooking mussels
- **4** tablespoons unsalted butter
- **½** cup chopped fresh parsley leaves

Master Instructions

1. Bring wine, shallots, garlic, and bay leaf to simmer in large pot. Continue to simmer to blend flavors for about 3 minutes. Increase heat to high and add clams or mussels. Cover and cook, stirring twice, until clams or mussels open, 4 to 8 minutes, depending on size of shellfish and pot.

2. Use slotted spoon to transfer clams or mussels to large serving bowl. Swirl butter into pan liquid to make emulsified sauce. Stir in parsley. Pour broth over clams or mussels and serve immediately.

▞ VARIATIONS:

Steamed Clams or Mussels with White Wine, Curry, and Herbs

Follow Master Recipe, adding 1 teaspoon curry powder to simmering liquid in step 1. Right after swirling in butter, stir in 2 tablespoons each chopped fresh cilantro and basil leaves and reduce parsley to 2 tablespoons.

Steamed Clams or Mussels with White Wine, Tomato, and Basil

This may be served over one pound of cooked linguine if desired.

Follow Master Recipe, decreasing wine to 1 cup. Once clams or mussels have been removed from broth, add 2 cups crushed canned tomatoes along with ¼ cup olive oil in place of butter. Simmer until reduced to sauce consistency, about 10 minutes. Substitute basil for parsley. Season with salt and pepper. Return clams or mussels to pot, heat briefly, and serve immediately.

Steamed Clams or Mussels with Asian Flavors

Follow Master Recipe, omitting ingredient list except for clams or mussels. Instead, steam shellfish in 1 cup chicken stock, 2 tablespoons soy or fish sauce, 2 teaspoons vinegar (preferably rice), ⅛ teaspoon cayenne pepper, 2 tablespoons minced fresh gingerroot, 4 minced scallions (green and white parts), and 1 tablespoon grated lime zest. Garnish with 2 tablespoons chopped fresh cilantro leaves, 2 tablespoons minced chives or scallions, and lime quarters.

Mussels Steamed in Beer
Follow Master Recipe, using mussels and substituting light-colored beer for wine and one small onion for shallots. Add 3 sprigs fresh thyme to beer along with onion, garlic, and bay leaf.

Steamed Mussels with Cream Sauce and Tarragon
Follow Master Recipe using mussels. After removing mussels from pot, simmer cooking liquid until reduced to ½ cup, about 8 minutes. Add ¾ cup heavy cream and reduce until thickened, about 2 minutes. Omit butter. Stir in parsley, 2 teaspoons minced fresh tarragon leaves, and 1 tablespoon lemon juice.

Grilled Clams or Mussels

➤ **NOTE:** *When the grill is on, we often like to throw clams or mussels over the coals and grill them just until they open. Don't move the shellfish around too much or you risk spilling the liquor out of the shells. This cooking method delivers pure clam or mussel flavor. If you like, serve with lemon wedges, a bottle of Tabasco or other hot sauce, and some fresh tomato salsa. Serves four as an appetizer.*

2 **pounds clams or mussels, scrubbed and debearded if cooking mussels**
Lemon wedges, hot sauce, and/or salsa

INSTRUCTIONS:

1. Light grill. When hot, place clams or mussels directly on cooking grate. Grill, without turning, until shellfish opens, 3 to 5 minutes for mussels and 6 to 10 minutes for clams.

2. With tongs, carefully transfer opened clams or mussels to flat serving platter, trying to preserve as much juice as possible. Discard top shells and loosen meat in bottom shell before serving if desired (*see* figure 7). Serve with lemon wedges, hot sauce, and/or salsa passed separately.

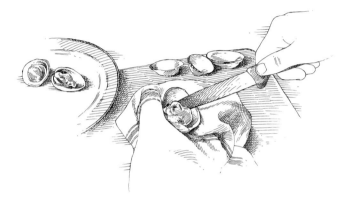

Figure 7.
The easiest way to serve grilled clams or mussels is to divide
them among small plates and give each person a small fork.
However, if you want guests to eat the clams or mussels right off
the shell, hold each one in a kitchen towel as you take it off the
grill, pull off and discard the top shell, then slide a paring knife
under the meat to detach it from the bottom shell. By the time
you have done this to each clam or mussel, the shells should have
cooled enough to permit everyone to pick them up and slurp the
meat directly from the shells.

chapter four

ᕹ

OYSTERS ON
THE HALF
SHELL

O FAVORITE WAY TO SERVE OYSTERS IS ON THE half shell. This is the best way to showcase their intense and exotic flavors. Oysters may be cooked in a stew or stuffed and baked, but we find that these preparations diminish the traits we like best about oysters. Serving oysters on the half shell also allows you to appreciate the stunning differences in oyster varieties.

It's easy to become overwhelmed by oysters. As if they weren't challenging enough to open, there are so many kinds it's hard to figure out what to buy. Walk into a good seafood shop and you may find Gliddens from Maine, Wellfleets from Massachusetts, Chincoteagues from Virginia, and Kumamotos from the West Coast. What's the difference and which should you buy?

The first thing to know is that there are only five species of oysters seen in the United States (*see* figure 8, page 58). The three most important are the familiar Atlantic, grown all along the East and Gulf coasts; the European, grown in the Northwest and a few spots in the far Northeast; and the Pacific, grown all along the West Coast. In addition, there are Olympias, oysters the size of a half-dollar that are indigenous to the Northwest and rarely seen elsewhere, and the trendy Kumamotos, once considered a variety of Pacific oyster but recently declared a distinct species.

The problem for shoppers is that within each of the three most popular species there are myriad nicknames and place names: The Atlantic is not only called the Eastern but is casually referred to by many place names (such as Wellfleet and Chincoteague); the European is known as the "flat" and also—incorrectly—as the belon, a name that belongs to oysters from a small region in France; and the Pacific, which is also grown in Europe, not only has place names attached to it but is sometimes called a Portuguese ("Portugaise"), after a now-extinct species that once made up the majority of oysters grown in Europe.

All this nomenclature business would be fodder only for linguists if oysters did not taste so different from one and another. An oyster from the mainland-facing side of Martha's Vineyard and one from the Atlantic side, for example, taste as different as two good but distinct bottles of Napa Valley Merlot. In fact, oysters are quite a bit like wine: You have the species, which corresponds to the grape variety, and the specific oysters from each location, which correspond to individual wines. Climate, water quality, and the age and condition of the growing beds are among the factors that affect the taste of an individual oyster.

Nevertheless, just as all Merlots have some things in common, so do all oysters from a particular species. To describe the major attributes of each species, we had more than a dozen people taste 13 kinds of oysters from all over the country. Here are the general conclusions from our panel's tasting notes.

■ ATLANTIC OYSTERS Crisp and briny, with a fresh, cold flavor of salt, and lightly fishy. Easy to like and not complex. Range in size from 2 inches to nearly 6 when grown in warm southern waters. We preferred crisp, brinier oysters (Wellfleets, Blue Points, etc.) from cold northern waters. Southern oysters (Chincoteagues, Apalachicholas, etc.) were softer, flabbier, and not nearly as briny.

PACIFIC OYSTERS Rarely salty but very complex tasting and often fruity. (Many tasters compared the flavor with cucumber or watermelon.) Sometimes sweet or even muddy. Our tasters preferred them sweet rather than muddy tasting. Usually 3 to 4 inches long.

EUROPEAN OR FLAT OYSTERS Very challenging and off-putting to oyster novices. When good, they start out tasting crisp and briny (like an Atlantic), but the finish is strong and metallic—something many oyster connoisseurs love. These oysters are round and measure about 5 inches in diameter.

KUMAMOTOS Very appealing because they combine the complexity of the Pacific oyster with more sweetness and less muddiness. Can be briny in the same way as good Atlantics. Because they're fairly small, they can be eaten in one bite.

OLYMPIAS Very hard to find outside of the Northwest. If you do find them, they are usually briny and metallic, much like flats. Very small.

In addition to considering species, pay close attention to freshness and season when shopping. The best oyster is the freshest. Older oysters are drier, flabbier, and less flavorful. Merchants are required by law to keep the tags that come with each container of oysters. The tag shows the place of origin and date of harvest. A reputable fishmonger can tell you exactly where and when an oyster was harvested. Any oysters more than a few days old should not be purchased.

Season is also key. The old adage about not eating oysters during months that don't contain the letter *R* is not as important as it used to be, when people spurned oysters in the summer because they died more quickly out of the water. But many oysters do spawn in the months without an *R*—May, June, July, and August—and spawning makes the meat mushy and less appetizing.

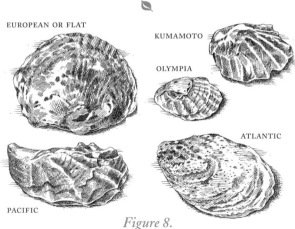

EUROPEAN OR FLAT

KUMAMOTO

OLYMPIA

ATLANTIC

PACIFIC

Figure 8.
The five types of oysters.

Shucked Oysters with Champagne Dressing

➤ NOTE: *Purists serve shucked oysters as is or with a squirt of lemon juice and a sprinkling of pepper. We also like oysters with a simple champagne dressing. Avoid dressings that contain oil (it makes the oysters greasy) or that are overly acidic or harsh. We liked champagne vinegar best but also recommend white wine or rice vinegar. In any case, use a high-quality vinegar. The right oyster knife is essential for opening oysters quickly and safely. (For more information, see page 60.) Serves four to six.*

½ cup good quality champagne vinegar
1 teaspoon coarsely ground black pepper
1 tablespoon minced shallot
Crushed ice
2 dozen fresh oysters

INSTRUCTIONS:

1. Combine vinegar, pepper, and shallot in small bowl and let sit a few minutes to let flavors mingle.

2. Meanwhile, arrange crushed ice on large platter. Shuck oysters (*see* figures 10 through 13, pages 62 and 63), being careful to keep oyster liquor in shells. Discard top shells. Carefully nestle oysters into ice. Serve with champagne dressing on the side.

BUYING AN OYSTER KNIFE

If you want to open more than one oyster every 10 minutes and end up with the shell, your temper, and your hands intact, it's important to have the right oyster knife. To find the best oyster knife, we had experienced and novice shuckers test several knives as well as a simple church-key can opener, which some experts claim is the best tool for the job.

Our two favorites were the Oxo (*see* figure 9) and the Dexter Russell S121. Both knives have blades with a slightly angled, pointed tip that makes it surprisingly easy to make that first penetration into the hinge between the top and bottom shells (*see* figure 10, page 62). The handles on these knives are also nicely contoured and textured for a secure, comfortable grip. Lastly, both knives have a long blade that makes it easy to detach the oyster meat once the shell has been pried open.

When an oyster knife is nowhere to be found, the pointed end of a church-key can opener will eventually open some oysters, but not without some heartache. (Church keys are common openers about the size of a stick of gum, often with a bottle opener on one end and a V-shaped can opener on the other.) We opened some oysters this way (it took two or three times as long), but others never yielded to this crude substitute for a real oyster knife.

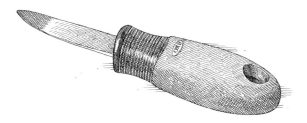

Figure 9.
This oyster knife (made by Oxo) has a slightly angled,
pointed tip that makes it easy to open the hinge between the top
and bottom shells. The blade is long enough to detach the oyster
meat from the shell, and the handle is contoured for a secure,
comfortable grip.

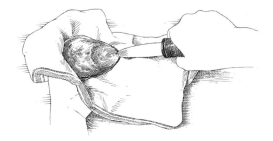

Figure 10.
Shucking an oyster is easy if you have the right tool (see page 61)
and technique. Remember to keep the oyster flat as you work to
keep the flavorful juices from spilling out of the shell. Start by
holding the oyster cupped side down in a kitchen towel. Locate
the hinge with the tip of the knife.

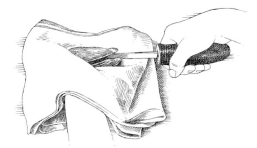

Figure 11.
Push between the edges of shells, wiggling back and forth
to pry them open.

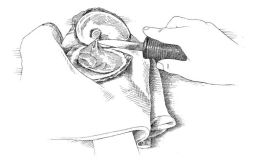

Figure 12.
Detach the meat from the top shell and discard the shell.

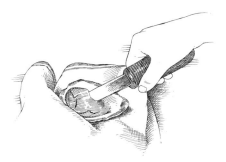

Figure 13.
To make eating easier, sever the muscle that holds the meat
of the oyster to the bottom shell.

63

chapter five

LOBSTER

S WITH CLAMS AND MUSSELS, WE FOUND that shopping for lobster is just as important as cooking. Lobsters must be purchased alive. Choose lobsters that are active in the tank, avoiding listless specimens that may have been in the tank too long. Maine lobsters (which are actually found on the northeast coast from Canada to New Jersey), with their large claws, are meatier and sweeter than clawless rock or spiny lobsters. They are our first choice. Size is really a matter of preference and budget. We found it possible to cook large as well as small lobsters to perfection as long as we adjusted the cooking time (*see* page 70).

During our initial phase of testing, we confirmed our preference for steamed lobster rather than boiled. Steamed lobster did not taste better than boiled, but the process was simpler and neater, and the finished product was less watery when cracked open on the plate. Steaming the lobster on a rack or steamer basket kept it from becoming waterlogged. (If you happen to live near the ocean, seaweed makes a natural rack.) We found that additions to the pot—beer, wine, herbs, spices, or other seasonings—failed to improve the lobster's flavor. It seems that nothing can penetrate the hard lobster shell.

As for dry-heat cooking methods, we found the steady, even heat of the oven preferable to broiling, where charring of the meat is a real danger. We found that a high oven temperature of 450 degrees works the best. You want to cook the lobster quickly. When we roasted lobsters at lower temperatures, the outer layer of meat had dried out by the time the inside was cooked through. To keep the tail from curling during roasting, we found it helpful to run a skewer through it (*see* figure 22, page 75).

Although we had little trouble perfecting these two cooking methods, we were bothered by the toughness of some of the lobsters tails we were eating. No matter how we cooked them, most of the tails were at least slightly rubbery and chewy.

We spent six months talking to research scientists, chefs, seafood experts, lobstermen, and home cooks to see how they tackled the problem of the tough tail. The suggestions ranged from the bizarre (petting the lobster to "hypnotize" it and thus prevent an adrenaline rush at death that causes the tail to toughen, or using a chopstick to kill the lobster before cooking) to the sensible (avoiding really old, large lobsters). But after testing every one of these suggestions, we still didn't have a cooking method that consistently delivered a tender tail.

Occasionally, we would get a nice tender tail, but there did not seem to a pattern. We then spoke with several scientists who said we were barking up the wrong tree. The secret to tender lobster was not so much in the preparation and cooking as in the selection.

Before working on this topic in the test kitchen, the terms *hard-shell* and *soft-shell* lobster meant nothing to us. Unlike crabs, there's certainly no distinction between the two at the retail level. Of course, we knew from past experience that some lobster claws rip open as easily an aluminum flip-top can, while others require shop tools to crack. We also noticed the wimpy, limp claw meat of some lobsters and the full, packed meat of others. We attributed these differences to the length of time the lobsters had been stored in tanks. It seems we were wrong. These variations

66

are caused by the particular stage of molting that the lobster is in at the time it is caught.

As it turns out, most of the lobsters we eat during the summer and fall are in some phase of molting. During the late spring, as waters begin to warm, lobsters start to form the new shell tissue underneath their old shells. As early as June off the shores of New Jersey and in July or August in colder Maine and Canadian waters, the lobsters shed their hard exterior shell. Because the most difficult task in molting is pulling the claw muscle through the old shell, the lobster dehydrates its claw (hence the smaller, wimpier claw meat).

Once the lobster molts, it emerges with nothing but a wrinkled, soft covering, much like that on a soft-shell crab. Within 15 minutes, the lobster inflates itself with water, increasing its length by 15 percent and its weight by 50 percent. This extra water expands the wrinkled, soft covering, allowing the lobster room to grow long after the shell starts to harden. The newly molted lobster immediately eats its old shell, digesting the crucial shell-hardening calcium.

Understanding the molt phase clarifies the deficiencies of soft-shell summer lobster. It explains why it so water-logged, why its claw meat is so shriveled and scrawny, and why its tail meat is so underdeveloped and chewy. A one-pound soft-shell lobster also has far less meat than a one-pound hard-shell lobster. (*See* page 70 for more details.)

During the fall, the lobster shell continues to harden and the meat expands to fill the new shell. By spring, lobsters are at their peak, packed with meat and relatively inexpensive since it is easier for fishermen to check their traps than it is during the winter. As the tail grows, it becomes firmer and meatier and will cook up tender, not tough. Better texture and more meat are two excellent reasons to give lobsters a squeeze at the market (*see* figure 14) and buy only those with hard shells. As a rule thumb, hard-shell lobsters are reasonably priced from Mother's Day through the Fourth of July.

Figure 14.

Hard-shell lobsters are much meatier than soft-shell lobsters, which have recently molted. To determine whether a lobster has a hard or soft shell, squeeze the side of the lobster's body. A soft-shell lobster will yield to pressure, while a hard-shell lobster will feel hard, brittle, and tightly packed.

Steamed Lobsters

➤ **N O T E :** *Because hard-shell lobsters are packed with more meat than soft-shell lobsters, you may want to buy slightly larger lobsters if the shells appear to be soft. Serves four.*

4   whole lobsters

8   tablespoons unsalted butter, melted until hot
     (optional)
     Lemon wedges

I N S T R U C T I O N S :

Bring about 1 inch of water to boil over high heat in a large soup kettle set up with wire rack, pasta insert, or seaweed bed. Add lobsters, cover, and return water to boil. Reduce heat to medium-high and steam until lobsters are done (*see* chart on page 70). Serve immediately with warm butter and lemon wedges.

Approximate Steaming Times and Meat Yields

LOBSTER SIZE	COOKING TIME *(in minutes)*	MEAT YIELD *(in ounces)*
1 lb		
soft-shell	8 to 9	about 3
hard-shell	10 to 11	4 to 4½
1¼ lbs		
soft-shell	11 to 12	3½ to 4
hard-shell	13 to 14	5½ to 6
1½ lbs		
soft-shell	13 to 14	5½ to 6
hard-shell	15 to 16	7½ to 8
1¾ -2 lbs		
soft-shell	17 to 18	6¼ to 6½
hard-shell	about 19	8½ to 9

Oven-Roasted Lobsters with Herbed Bread Crumbs

➤ **NOTE:** *Freezing the lobster for 10 minutes numbs the creature and makes it easier to handle when cutting in half for roasting. Freezing for this short amount of time does not affect the texture or quality of the meat. Serves four.*

4	tablespoons unsalted butter
½	cup plain dry bread crumbs
2	tablespoons minced fresh parsley leaves or 1 tablespoon minced fresh tarragon leaves or snipped chives
4	whole lobsters, prepared according to steps 15 through 22, pages 72 to 75 Salt and ground black pepper Lemon wedges

⠿ INSTRUCTIONS:

1. Adjust oven rack to middle-high position and heat oven to 450 degrees. Heat 1 tablespoon butter in small skillet over medium heat. When foaming subsides, add bread crumbs and cook, stirring occasionally, until toasted and golden brown, 3 to 4 minutes. Stir in herbs and set aside.

2. Arrange lobsters crosswise on two 17-by-11-inch foil-lined jelly roll pans, alternating tail and claw ends. Melt

71

remaining butter and brush over body and tail of each lobster; season with salt and pepper to taste. Sprinkle portion of bread crumb mixture evenly over body and tail meat.

3. Roast lobsters until tail meat is opaque and bread crumbs are crisp, 12 to 15 minutes. Serve immediately with lemon wedges.

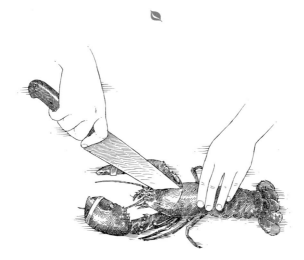

Figure 15.

Place the lobster in the freezer for 10 minutes to numb it. With the blade of a chef's knife facing the head, kill the lobster by plunging the knife into the body at the point where the shell forms a "T." Move the blade down until it touches the head.

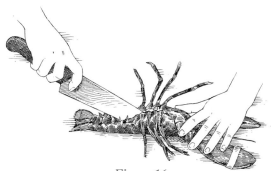

Figure 16.
Turn the lobster over, then, holding the upper body with one
hand and positioning the knife blade so that it faces the tail end,
cut through the body toward the tail, making sure not to cut
all the way through the shell.

Figure 17.
Move your hand down to the lower body and continue cutting
through the tail.

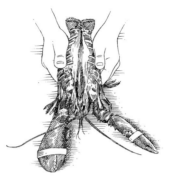

Figure 18.
Holding half of the tail in each hand, crack, but do not break,
the back shell to butterfly the lobster.

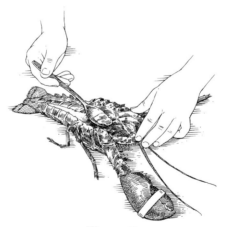

Figure 19.
Use a spoon to remove and discard the stomach sac.

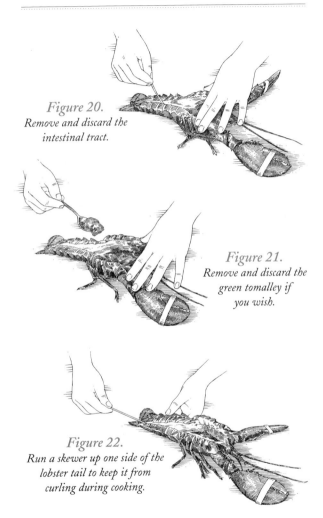

Figure 20.
Remove and discard the intestinal tract.

Figure 21.
Remove and discard the green tomalley if you wish.

Figure 22.
Run a skewer up one side of the lobster tail to keep it from curling during cooking.

chapter six

CRABS

THERE ARE DOZENS OF SPECIES OF CRABS, including stone crabs from Florida, king crabs from Alaska, and Dungeness crabs from the West Coast. The most widely available crab is the blue crab, which is found along the East Coast. Live blue crabs may be boiled and served as is. There's not much meat on a crab, and getting to it is a messy proposition. A crab boil is easy to prepare, but it's not the most efficient way to enjoy crabmeat. We think that a crab boil makes the most sense as an appetizer or part of a larger seafood spread, not as a main course. Thankfully, the meat is picked from the shell by processors and sold as fresh crabmeat when you need crabmeat in quantity for use in salads and crab cakes.

One of our favorite ways to consume blue crabs is when they are soft-shell crabs. Soft-shell crabs are blue crabs that have been taken out of the water just after they have shed their shells in the spring or summer. At this brief stage of its life, the whole crab, with its new, soft, gray skin, is almost completely edible and especially delicious. They should be purchased alive and cleaned at home for optimum flavor. Once cleaned, the crab should be cooked immediately.

To our way of thinking, the whole point of cooking soft-shells is to make them crisp. The legs should crunch delicately, while the body should provide a contrast between its thin, crisp outer skin and the soft, rich interior that explodes juicily in the mouth. Deep-frying delivers these results, but this method is better suited to restaurants. Air pockets and water in the crab cause a lot of dangerous splattering. For optimum safety, soft-shell crabs should be fried in a very large quantity of oil in a very deep pot, which is not practical at home.

We wanted to develop an alternative method for home cooks. We tried roasting, but the crabs didn't get crisp enough. Pan-frying lightly floured crabs produces a satisfyingly crisp crust. Crabs still splatter hot fat when cooked this way, but far less than when deep-fried. To avoid the mess and danger of the splattering hot fat, we recommend sliding a splatter screen (a round wire net with a handle) over the pan. We tried various coatings, including cornmeal, bread crumbs, and even Cream of Wheat. These coatings all detracted from the flavor of the crab. Flour produces a nice crisp crust with minimal effect on flavor.

We tried soaking the crabs in milk for two hours before applying the flour coating, a trick advocated by several sources to "sweeten" the meat. Again, we found that this method detracted from the fresh-out-of-the-water flavor of the crabs.

We also tried various fats for pan-frying, including whole butter, clarified butter, vegetable and peanut oils, and a combination of whole butter and olive oil. We found that whole butter gives the crabs a nutty flavor and browns them well. It is our recommended all-purpose cooking fat. Peanut oil produces especially crisp crabs. It does not add the rich flavor of butter, but works well when Asian flavorings are used to sauce the crabs.

We found that you need a tablespoon of fat for each crab and that a large skillet will accommodate only four crabs. Since two soft-shells make a typical serving, you will need two pans when cooking for four people. Although any heavy-bottomed skillet will work, cast iron holds heat especially well and is recommended.

Once the soft-shells have been cooked, they should be sauced and served immediately. Because the crabs are pan-fried, they don't need much of a sauce. A drizzle of something acidic, such as a squirt of lemon juice, is sufficient.

When shopping for soft-shells, look for fresh rather than frozen crabs. Most stores will offer to clean the crabs for you. Refuse their offer if you can. When you clean a live crab, it begins to lose its juices. In our tests, we found that a crab cooked immediately after cleaning is plumper and juicier than a crab cleaned several hours before cooking.

While soft-shells are certainly the easiest way to enjoy the flavor of crabs, there is something appealing about a crab boil. In our tests, we found that less is more here. The crabs have so much flavor that they can be boiled in plain water. You can add seasonings such as Old Bay if you like, but they are far from essential.

For those who don't like a mess or to work for their dinner, fresh crabmeat is a good, if expensive, alternative. Other forms of crabmeat just don't compare. Canned crabmeat is—well—horrible; like canned tuna, it bears little resemblance to the fresh product. Fresh pasteurized crabmeat is watery and bland. Frozen crabmeat is stringy and wet. There is no substitute for fresh blue crabmeat, preferably "jumbo lump," which indicates the largest pieces and highest grade.

For crab cakes and salads, fresh unpasteurized jumbo lump crabmeat is the only choice. For best flavor, don't rinse the crabmeat. Just pick over the meat to make sure all the cartilage and shell pieces have been removed.

Master Recipe

Pan-Fried Soft-Shell Crabs

➤ **NOTE**: *A splatter screen (see figure 26, page 85) is essential if you want to minimize the mess and the danger to your arms and face. For maximum crispness, you should cook the crabs in two pans, each covered with a splatter screen, so you can serve the crabs as soon as they are cooked. If you are working with just one splatter screen and pan, cook four crabs in four tablespoons of butter, transfer them to a platter in a 300-degree oven, wipe out the pan, add 4 more tablespoons of butter, and cook the remaining crabs. Serves four as a main course, eight as an appetizer.*

8	medium-to-large soft-shell crabs, cleaned (*see* figures 23 through 25, pages 83 and 84) and patted dry with paper towels
	All-purpose flour for dredging
10	tablespoons unsalted butter
¼	cup lemon juice
2	tablespoons minced fresh parsley leaves
	Ground black pepper

♛
Master Instructions

1. Dredge crabs in flour; pat off excess. Heat two 11- or 12-inch heavy-bottomed frying pans over medium-high heat until pans are quite hot, about 3 minutes. Add 4 tablespoons butter to each pan, swirling pans to keep butter from burning as it melts. When foam subsides, add four crabs, skins down, to each pan. Cover each pan with splatter screen and cook, adjusting heat as necessary to keep butter from burning, until crabs turn reddish brown, about 3 minutes. Turn crabs with spatula or tongs and cook until second side is browned, about 3 minutes more. Drain crabs on plate lined with paper towel.

2. Set one pan aside. Discard the butter in the other pan and remove from heat. Add lemon juice to that pan to deglaze it. Cut remaining 2 tablespoons butter into pieces and add to skillet. Swirl pan to melt butter. Add parsley and salt and pepper to taste. Arrange two crabs on each of four plates. Spoon some sauce over each plate and serve immediately.

▪▪ **VARIATIONS:**

Pan-Fried Soft-Shell Crabs with Lemon, Capers, and Herbs

The pan sauce is tart and powerfully flavorful; you need only about one tablespoon per serving.

Follow Master Recipe through step 1. Set one pan aside and discard the butter in the other pan. Off heat, add 3 tablespoons lemon juice, 2 teaspoons sherry vinegar, 1½ teaspoons drained and chopped capers, and 1 minced scallion. Swirl in butter as directed in Master Recipe. Add 2 teaspoons minced fresh tarragon along with parsley, salt, and pepper. Spoon sauce over crabs and serve.

Pan-Fried Soft-Shelled Crabs with Orange and Soy

This Asian recipe uses peanut oil rather than butter to cook the crabs.

Follow Master Recipe, using ¼ cup peanut oil in each pan in step 1. When crabs are done, remove and drain as directed. Set one pan aside and discard the oil in the other pan. Add 2 tablespoons fresh peanut oil to pan and return to medium heat. Add 3 medium minced garlic cloves, ¾ teaspoon minced fresh gingerroot, and ¼ teaspoon hot red pepper flakes, and sauté until garlic is fragrant and lightened in color, 30 to 45 seconds. Off heat, stir in 2 tablespoons orange juice, 2 tablespoons rice vinegar, 1 teaspoon soy sauce, and 2 thinly sliced scallions. Spoon sauce over crabs and serve.

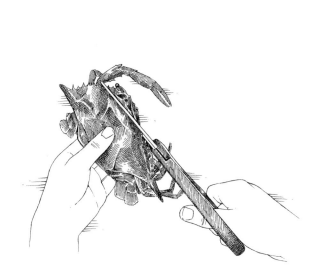

Figure 23.
To clean a soft-shell crab, first cut off its mouth with kitchen
scissors; the mouth is the first part of the shell to harden.
You can also cut off the eyes at the same time, but this is purely
for aesthetic reasons since the eyes are edible.

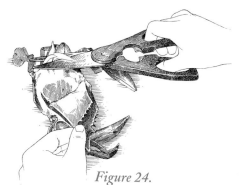

Figure 24.

Next, lift the pointed side of the crab and cut out the spongy off-white gills underneath; the gills are fibrous and watery and unpleasant to eat.

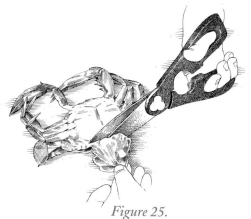

Figure 25.

Finally, turn the crab on its back and cut off the triangular, or T-shaped, "apron flap."

84

Figure 26.
Because they are full of water, soft-shells spit hot fat like crazy
when fried. To protect your hands and face (and to keep your
stove top from becoming covered with grease), slide a splatter
screen—a round wire net with a handle—over the pan with the
crabs as they cook. Steam can escape through the netting so the
crabs stay crisp, and the fat stays in the pan.

Master Recipe

Boiled Blue Crabs

➤ **NOTE**: *We find that crabs have so much flavor they are best boiled in plain water. You can add seasonings (see the variations), but they are far from essential. An 8-quart stock pot will hold only 8 crabs at a time. If you want to cook more crabs, keep reusing the liquid as needed. Or, if you like, use a larger pot and more water, following the proportions outlined in this recipe. Eating boiled crabs (see figures 27 through 30, pages 88 and 89) is a lot of work, and we think they make more sense as an appetizer than a main course. Serves four as an appetizer.*

8   blue crabs (6 to 8 ounces each), rinsed
     Lemon wedges

▓ **INSTRUCTIONS**:

Bring 4½ quarts water to boil in 8-quart stock pot. Using tongs, add crabs and boil until bright orange-red, about 5 minutes. Remove crabs with tongs and serve with lemon wedges.

▚ VARIATIONS:

Crab Boil with Vinegar and Old Bay

Bring 4 quarts water, 2 cups white vinegar, and 1 tablespoon Old Bay to boil in pot. Cook crabs as directed and serve with lemon wedges.

Spicy Crab Boil with Vinegar and Old Bay

Bring 4 quarts water, 2 cups white vinegar, 1 tablespoon Old Bay, 1 teaspoon cayenne, and 1 tablespoon paprika to boil in pot. Cook crabs as directed and serve with lemon wedges.

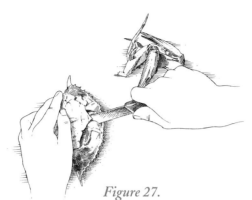

Figure 27.

Eating whole blue crabs can be a challenge. Start by twisting off the claws and legs and breaking them open with a mallet or crackers to expose the meat. Once all the claws and legs have been detached, turn the crab upside-down and insert a paring knife into the front of the crab. Twist the knife to loosen the bottom shell from the rest of the crab.

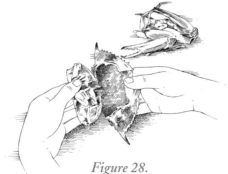

Figure 28.

Remove the knife and pry the bottom shell (at left above) off the body of the crab. Discard the top shell.

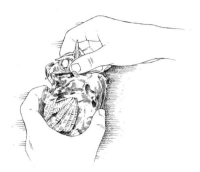

Figure 29.
Use your fingers to remove the feathery, white gills on either side
of the crab.

Figure 30.
Use your hands to break the crab in half front to back. Break each
piece in half again to expose the meat of the crab.

Pan-Fried Crab Cakes

➤ **NOTE:** *The amount of bread crumbs you add will depend on the crabmeat's juiciness. Start with the smallest amount, adjust the seasonings, and then add the egg. If the cakes won't bind at this point, then add more bread crumbs, one tablespoon at a time. You want to avoid adding too much filling, which will mask the flavor of the crabs. Chilling the shaped cakes is essential; it helps them keep their shape when cooked and reduces the amount of binder necessary. Serves four.*

1	pound jumbo lump crabmeat, picked over to remove cartilage and shell
4	scallions, green part only, minced (about ½ cup)
1	tablespoon chopped fresh herb, such as cilantro, dill, basil, or parsley
1½	teaspoons Old Bay seasoning
2 to 4	tablespoons plain dry bread crumbs
¼	cup mayonnaise Salt and ground white pepper
1	large egg
¼	cup all-purpose flour
¼	cup vegetable oil

⠿ **INSTRUCTIONS:**

1. Gently mix crabmeat, scallions, herb, Old Bay, 2 table-spoons bread crumbs, and mayonnaise in medium bowl, being

9 0

careful not to break up crab lumps. Season with salt and pepper to taste. Carefully fold in egg with rubber spatula just until mixture clings together. Add more crumbs if necessary.

2. Divide crab mixture into four portions and shape each into a fat, round cake about 3 inches across and 1½ inches high. Arrange on baking sheet lined with waxed paper; cover with plastic wrap and chill for at least 30 minutes. (Can be refrigerated up to 24 hours.)

3. Put flour on plate or in pie tin. Lightly dredge crab cakes. Heat oil in large, preferably nonstick skillet over medium-high heat until hot but not smoking. Gently lay chilled crab cakes in skillet. Pan-fry, turning once, until outsides are crisp and browned, 4 to 5 minutes per side. Serve hot, with Tartar Sauce (page 92) or Creamy Dipping Sauce (page 93) if desired.

Tartar Sauce

➤ **NOTE:** *This is the classic sauce for crab cakes and fried seafood. It is delicious with either prepared or homemade mayo. Makes generous ¾ cup.*

¾	cup mayonnaise
1½	tablespoons minced cornichons (about 3 large), plus 1 teaspoon cornichon juice
1	tablespoon minced scallion
1	tablespoon minced red onion
1	tablespoon drained capers, minced

INSTRUCTIONS:

Mix all ingredients in small bowl. Cover and refrigerate until flavors blend, at least 30 minutes. (Can be refrigerated for several days.)

Creamy Dipping Sauce

➤ **NOTE:** *The chipotle gives this sauce some mild chile heat. This sauce can be used with crab cakes or any fried seafood. Makes about ½ cup.*

¼	cup mayonnaise
¼	cup sour cream
2	teaspoons minced chipotle chiles
1	small garlic clove, minced
2	teaspoons minced fresh cilantro leaves
1	teaspoon lime juice

INSTRUCTIONS:

Mix all ingredients in small bowl. Cover and refrigerate until flavors blend, at least 30 minutes. (Can be refrigerated for several days.)

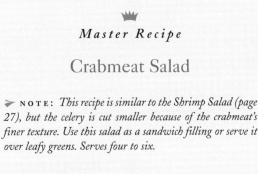

Master Recipe

Crabmeat Salad

➤ **NOTE:** *This recipe is similar to the Shrimp Salad (page 27), but the celery is cut smaller because of the crabmeat's finer texture. Use this salad as a sandwich filling or serve it over leafy greens. Serves four to six.*

1	pound jumbo lump crabmeat, picked over to remove cartilage or shell
1	medium celery rib, chopped fine
1	medium scallion, white and green parts, minced
⅓	cup mayonnaise
1	tablespoon lemon juice
1	tablespoon minced fresh parsley leaves
	Salt and ground black pepper

INSTRUCTIONS:

Mix all ingredients in medium bowl. Season with salt and pepper to taste. (Can be covered and refrigerated overnight.)

■■ **VARIATIONS:**

Crabmeat Salad with Lemon and Tarragon

Substitute 1 tablespoon minced fresh tarragon leaves for parsley and add 1 teaspoon grated lemon zest to mixture.

Crabmeat Salad with Chives and Horseradish

Substitute 2 tablespoon snipped chives for parsley and add ¾ teaspoon prepared horseradish. Omit scallion.

index